**SPALDING**

Guide to

*Better*
GOLF

# SPALDING

## Guide to

# *Better* GOLF

**Peter Croker**

Edited by Helen Wadsworth

PHOTOGRAPHS BY ROGER GOULD

## foulsham

LONDON · NEW YORK · TORONTO · SYDNEY

# foulsham

Yeovil Road, Slough, Berkshire SL1 4JH

Australia has always produced golf stars of quality, if not in quantity. Norman Von Nida, Peter Thomson, Kel Nagle, David Graham and Rodger Davies are among the most familiar of the Antipodean ambassadors, past and present.

But, a new breed of attacking player, spearheaded by Greg Norman, is invading the world's golf scene. Mike Clayton, Steve Elkington, Ian Baker-Finch, Ossie Moore, Craig Parry, Peter Fowler and Wayne Riley are just some of the new names establishing themselves in Europe and America.

Peter Croker, founder-director of Australian Golf Schools, has helped, in his own way, towards this explosion of talent. Twelve years as a tournament professional playing alongside the world's best players, and learning from the former greats, has given Croker a great base from which to teach.

Paul Runyan is one of those greats. Leading US money winner in 1933 and 1934 and USPGA champion in 1934 and 1938, he was known as 'Little Poison' because of his deadly putting. Renowned as a teacher, specialising in putting problems, Runyan's ageless advise has been passed through Croker in this invaluable instruction guide.

ISBN 0–572–01545–3
first published in 1987 by Lothian Publishing Company. Text © Peter Croker
Photographs © Roger Gould. This U.K. edition Copyright © 1989 W. Foulsham and Co. Ltd

Printed in Great Britain by St Edmundsbury Press Ltd, Bury St Edmunds, Suffolk

# CONTENTS

# FOREWORD BY PETER THOMSON

There are as many golf swings as there are golfers, and a mighty number of them successful at hitting a ball squarely, solidly in the right direction, with adequate power.

Our swings are as unique to us as our thumb print. We swing according to our stature, with a speed our muscles and sinews allow, and generally speaking we are stuck with that.

Yet we can improve our striking technique, improve results, and get better scores with sensible guidance such as Peter Croker presents in this book.

Croker has been a keen analyst of technique for many years, collecting data, impressions and images as he went. No one asked more questions of the game's finest players, or delved deeper into the thought behind the successful.

In professional golf there are both players and teachers. Some progress from the one to the other as Peter Croker has done, combining his personal experiences from competing at the top with the time he has spent instructing beginners and good players alike.

This seems to me a priceless apprenticeship for the role of lecturer and writer on the game of golf and the way it is played best.

Most great names in golf are tied up in total concentration on their own performance. Occasionally glossy books of instruction emerge divulging the great players' ''secrets'' of success. Such ghosted offerings are of limited use.

What is of lasting value, is an outline explained by a competent teacher in simple terms, that leads us, stage by stage, to a real understanding of what is vital to creative stroke play, and what will stand us in good stead when ''the chips are down''.

It is never too late to learn and I commend this book of explanation and advice. It comes from a man whose heart is in it and who is bursting to pass it on to others.

Peter Thomson,
San Antonio,
6 May 1987.

# ACKNOWLEDGMENTS

To Spalding Australia for co-operation and support. To Peter Thomson for so kindly providing the Foreword. To John Ross and Garry Mansfield for their encouragement and advice on the book's presentation. To Patterson River Country Club for the use of their wonderful course as the background for the pictures used to illustrate the golf swing. To Roger Gould, one of Australia's best sports photographers, for his clear and precise photos.

# INTRODUCTION

To improve and learn how to play golf well is within reach of anyone. Indeed, it is the challenge to improve that captivates most players. But golf is not a simple game. It is complex, requires a little thinking and a lot of hard work.

The aim of this book is to show you how to improve. It progresses through the fundamentals and towards a golf swing of effortless power (not powerless effort).

When learning how to swing the club, the conscious mind interferes with any natural movement and inconsistent results will occur. Be patient and trust the logic of these fundamentals. Golf is learned by direct mechanics but once the muscle memory patterns are learned more energy and time can be afforded to the art of scoring.

Golf is a great character builder and, like the swing, golfing character can be learned. Through true understanding of the fundamentals of all types of golf shots, from putting to driving, you can cope with poor shots knowing that you can make the next shot a good one. This book will help you reach that certainty.

Through the use of many photographs and a minimum of words I have aimed to give you true understanding of the simple basics of the golf swing. Any book introduces new thoughts, but it is hard for them to be speedily understood. For this reason I urge you to consult a competent teaching professional to guide your progress. Also regular reference to this book will expand your understanding.

In my golfing life I have learned directly from many great players. Peter Thomson, Norman Von Nida, Ben Hogan, Gary Player, Lee Trevino, Sam Snead and Seve Ballesteros have all been of great help in my understanding of the simplicity of the golf swing. Many have experienced the excitement of discovery and subsequent pleasure in golf which has motivated me to write this book.

Paul Runyan was a great inspiration to me. I was introduced to him through his book after 12 years on the tour and, realizing the greatness of his short game method, I searched him out to learn more. Many of the short game methods explained in this book are derived from the Runyan method.

I have always approached learning golf as an adventure, and with a positive expectancy that I am becoming a better golfer as time passes. Join me to help you learn the concepts of the swing, expand your understanding of golf and, above all, improve.

Good golfing
Peter Croker

# I
# THE FUNDAMENTALS

# THE SWING CONCEPT

1. The aim of the golf swing is to swing the clubhead in a circular motion around a steady centre at speed.
   This circular path resembles a cartwheel on an inclined plane.
   The centre of the wheel is at the base of the neck.
   The arms and club shaft represent the spokes in the wheel.
   The backbone represents the axle.
   The axle is connected to a motor (the hips).
   The motor is a rotary motor (the hips turn in a barrel).
2. The clubhead is swung in a circular orbit like swinging a brick on the end of a string.
   The energy is supplied from the centre out to keep the clubhead in orbit.

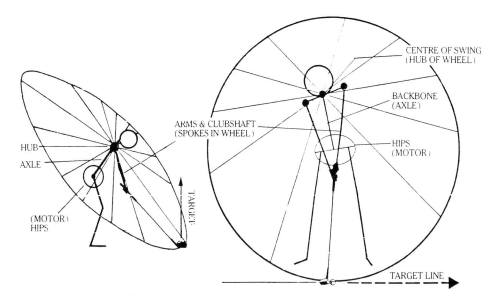

3. To swing the clubhead back, the motor (hips) turns the axle (backbone), the axle spins the wheel and the clubhead is dragged into a swinging motion.
   To swing the clubhead down and through, the motor (hips) reverses direction turning the axle (backbone) anti clockwise. The axle spins the wheel back spinning the arms, hands and clubhead down and through the ball.
4. A good swing is built on the geometry of the circle and the physics of rotation. In this way power is generated.
5. While the hips move the shoulders, arms, hands and club, back and through, they also move the legs and feet. Therefore, one correct move from the hips sets up a chain of actions above and below.
6. Wrist action multiplies clubhead speed throughout the swing. It helps the clubhead to swing the arms and shoulders back, and through to the finish.

**Dynamic balance** My simplest and perhaps best swing concept relates to balance in motion.

**At address** the weight is predominantly on the balls of my feet (not the heels).

**At the top of the backswing** the weight is on the back foot, the shoulder turn is flat and the golfer feels wound up around the back foot.

**At the finish** the weight is on the front foot, the head is up and over the front foot. The shoulder turn is flat and level.

**SUMMARY** Golf is a hips and hands, not an arms and shoulders, game.

# MUSCULAR ATTITUDE

To swing the club freely around a steady centre it is very important to have the correct muscle tension in the different muscle groups that co-ordinate to give the golfer a swing of effortless power, not powerless effort.

The muscle groups of importance are:

**1. Legs and hips** The lower body generates the initial force in the backswing and downswing and supports the swinging motion of the upper body, arms, hands and club. Therefore, you feel heavy in the feet and a springy, live tension in the legs and hips.

**2. The back and trunk muscles** These are braced for a straight back but are relaxed enough to allow a full turn back and through.

**3. Upper arms and shoulders** Totally relaxed to allow for a free swing. Arms hang like a gorilla.

**4. Hands and forearms** Relaxed and soft yet the fingers grip firmly.

1. GORILLA-ARMS HANGING     2. SWIMMER ON THE BLOCKS — SPRINGY IN THE LEGS.

# THE GRIP

The grip is the foundation of a free wheeling, uncompensated swing that hits the ball straight and true.

The hands are your only connection to the club and therefore must give you the feel of:

1. the weight of the club
2. the path of the swing
3. the direction of the club face
4. the speed and tempo of the swing

For the free wheeling uncompensated swing — our ideal model — the hands must be placed on the club in a neutral position i.e. the palms, if opened, would be parallel and at right angles to the swing path.

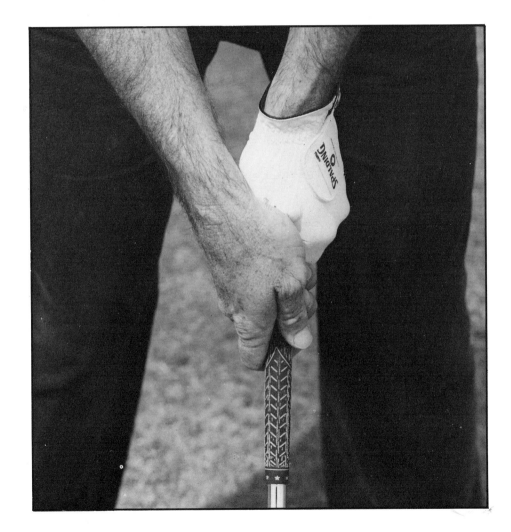

Looking down from the golfer's viewpoint.

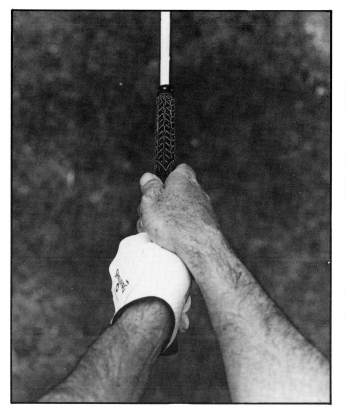

The two hands are placed together and will act as one unit.

Depending on the size of your hands and for your comfort, the grip can have either the little finger of the left hand interlocked with the forefinger of the right hand, or over lapped. Alternatively, all the fingers on both hands can be placed on the club to form the baseball grip.

OVERLAPPING GRIP

INTERLOCKING GRIP

BASEBALL GRIP  **13**

**LEFT HAND:** Point back of left hand at target. Club face points at target also. Grip touches hand at crease above little finger and runs diagonally across hand to first joint of index finger.

Fold fingers around grip with thumb on top right hand side. Pad of hand wedges grip mostly in fingers.

Looking down you see two/three knuckles. (If you are strongly built two knuckles, if light two/three knuckles.) The V between thumb and forefinger points to right eye. Butt of club points to left groin.

Pressure is exerted in the last three fingers of the left hand. Light finger pressure is required for maximum speed and distance — firm up the last three fingers to hit softer cut shots.

1. HAND POINTS AT TARGET.

2. GRIP OF CLUB ACROSS LEFT HAND.

3. LIGHT PRESSURE FOR MAXIMUM SPEED AND DISTANCE.

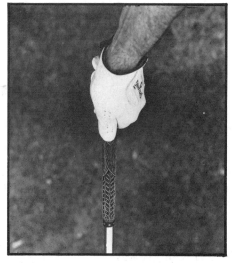
4. LOOKING DOWN YOU SEE TWO TO THREE KNUCKLES.

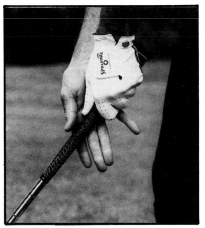

5. RIGHT HAND TOUCHES GRIP AT BASE OF INDEX FINGER.

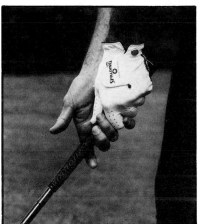

6. MIDDLE TWO FINGERS WRAP AROUND GRIP.

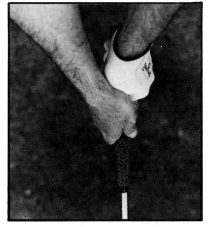

7. RIGHT HAND V POINTS TO RIGHT EYE.

**RIGHT HAND:** Open palm of right hand must be parallel to leading edge of club face and must face target.

Right hand touches grip at base of index finger.

Little finger overlaps between the index finger and second finger of left hand.

Middle two fingers wrap around grip. Hollow of palm of right hand covers the left thumb. The right thumb sits on the top left side of the grip. V formed by thumb and forefinger points at right eye. Two knuckles can also be seen as a further check.

Pressure points in the right hand are 1) the hollow of the palm of the right hand on the left thumb 2) the index finger on the grip.

1. PALMS PARALLEL TO LEADING EDGE OF CLUBFACE.
2. BACK OF LEFT HAND AND PALM OF RIGHT HAND AIMING AT TARGET.
3. CLUBFACE AIMING AT TARGET.

# THE ADDRESS POSITION

The address is the position the golfer puts himself into before hitting the ball. A good address position entails correct posture, correct feet and ball position, good weight distribution and accurate alignment. Whatever your build the following details should be observed.

**POSTURE** Posture involves how you set your body in relation to the ball and how your body weight is distributed.

1. A slight backward tilt puts the right shoulder lower than the left. The left arm is held straight but relaxed, the right arm is bent at the elbow and rests gently near the side. The arms hang from the shoulder socket (like a gorilla) with a little inner pressure bringing the elbows closer together.

2. There is slight pressure into the left hip and on the inside ball of the right foot.

3. The left upper arm presses firmly against the side of the chest forming approximately a 40 degree angle to the spine. This pressure point is maintained throughout the swing.

4. The feet, knees, hips and shoulders are all set parallel to the target line.

There are two bends of the body which are essential to good posture: the angle at the hips and the angle at the knees. To set these angles correctly, the back must be kept straight and the backside pushed outwards. The torso is bent forward from the waist so that the arms hang down loosely. The knees are flexed enough so that the vertical line extending down from the knee is over the balls of the feet. You should feel springy in the lower body and relaxed in the upper body and arms.

**FEET AND BALL POSITION** The feet are placed approximately shoulder width apart. The ball is positioned in the middle of the stance for the 5 iron through to the sand wedge, two inches inside the left heel for the long irons and off the inside front heel for the woods.

The line across the heels is parallel to the target line. The back foot is placed at right angles to the target line and the toe of the front foot turned slightly outward, away from the ball.

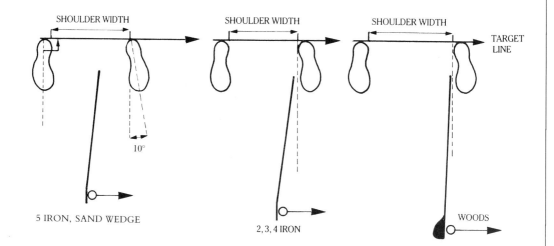

**WEIGHT DISTRIBUTION** For woods and long irons slightly more weight is placed on the inside of the right foot. For mid irons weight is placed evenly on both feet. For short irons slightly more weight is placed on the left side. To maximise stability throughout the swing the weight between the toes and the heels must be distributed evenly.

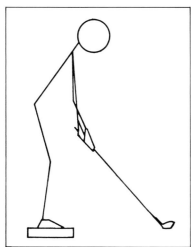

Weight evenly distributed between toes and heels for best balance. Feet feel flat and heavy (as though you have lead boots on)

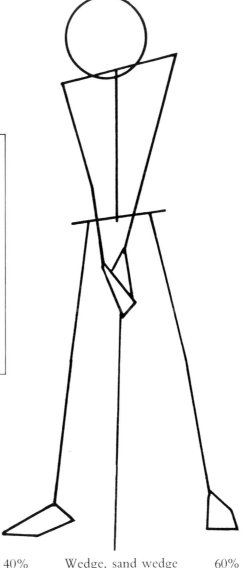

| 40% | Wedge, sand wedge | 60% |
| 45% | 7, 8, 9 irons | 55% |
| 50% | 5, 6 irons | 50% |
| 60% | Woods, long irons | 40% |

# II
## THE SWING

RIGHT SHOULDER BELOW LEFT
LEFT ARM STRAIGHT

# THE BACKSWING

**THE TAKEAWAY** Following the waggle and the forward press we move from the adjusted address position into the takeaway. Here the hip turn initiates the backward motion of the club in what appears a one piece movement. The hips turn horizontally, as if in a barrel, around the inside ball of the right foot. This constant weight positioning helps keep the right knee flexed and prevents the hips from overturning. The hips should turn no more than 45 degress. As the hips turn, the shoulders, arms, hands and club are dragged away smoothly without any active wrist action. The head remains in a quite central position. Because of the body turn, the clubface appears to open. In fact, the clubface closes slightly as the fingers of the left hand turn under to produce a flat left wrist early in the backswing. (A flat left wrist allows the hands to lead through impact.)

**WRIST COCK** When the hands are about waist high, and the clubhead is between knee high and waist high, the swinging club begins to exert a force on the wrists and causes them to hinge.

Remember that the grip on the club allows the wrists to cock in an oily fluid motion. Following the wristcock the arms swing upward and around in response to the body rotation and the club's momentum.

**THE TOP OF THE BACKSWING** The full backswing is complete when the body, arms and wrists have made as full a movement backwards as possible under the following constraints.

The head remains in a central position with the left arm straight, but not rigid. The grip remains unaltered and the wrists fully cocked. The weight remains on the inside ball of the right foot.

WAGGLE        ADDRESS        TAKEAWAY

The aim of these photo sequences is to highlight the circular motion and to show when and where wristcock occurs.

It must be stressed that the backswing is initiated by the hip turn and active, responding hands help complete the winding up of all the power in the backswing.

The backswing is where the power is built up. The hips coil against the feet. The wrists coil against the arms. The arms coil across the chest. The shoulders coil

THE WAGGLE        THE ADDRESS        THE TAKEAWAY

24

WRISTCOCK        WRISTCOCK AND ARM SWING        TOP OF BACKSWING

against the hips. This gives the full winding up of all the power around a steady centre.

Note that the backbone remains on the same inclined tilt from address to the top of the backswing.

The shoulders have turned as flat as possible.

When the club shaft is parallel to the ground at the top of the swing, the club should lie parallel to the target line.

WRISTCOCK        WRISTCOCK AND ARM SWING        TOP OF BACKSWING

| TOP OF BACKSWING | NEARING LATE RELEASE POINT | IMPACT |

# THE DOWNSWING, RELEASE AND FOLLOW THROUGH

Although these photos break up the swing into a number of phases, the golf swing itself is one complete motion. Therefore, it is to be emphasised that the downswing does not start from a stationary position — that is, there is no pause at the top of the swing.

## THE DOWNSWING

For a correct downswing to take place three moves must be made to blend together.

These are the movement of the hips, shoulders and arms.

**THE FIRST MOVEMENT — HOW THE HIPS MOVE** The downswing begins while the backswing of the arms is still in progress. The first movement, which initiates the downswing, is the turning of the left hip around the right hip.

| TOP OF BACKSWING | NEARING LATE RELEASE POINT | IMPACT |

| AFTER IMPACT | CROSSOVER | FINISH |

This left hip turn drives the left heel back firmly to the ground. The weight transfers dynamically to the left side.

As the left hip continues turning, the clubhead is thrown downward and outward by the force produced from flailing the left arm and club and by centrifugal force produced by the hip turn.

Note how little the shoulders turn in this complete area — from hip to hip. To this point the hips have turned to the maximum against the feet which are heavy in the ground. The left leg moves into a straightened position to produce a firm left side.

**THE SECOND MOVEMENT — HOW THE SHOULDERS MOVE** In response to the left hip turning left, *the left shoulder* resists slightly and in the process has a more vertical rotation. The left shoulder moves up, then around, keeping the hands on the 'inside path'.

**THE THIRD MOVEMENT — HOW THE ARMS MOVE** The arms move in response to the body in a downward motion with the butt of the left hand aiming at the ball. Imagine a string attached to the butt end of the club at the top of the backswing, passing through a pulley at the ball and back to attach to the left hip joint. As the hip turns left the string drags the hands toward the ball.

| AFTER IMPACT | CROSSOVER | FINISH |

| START DOWN | NEAR LATE RELEASE | RELEASE POINT | IMPACT |

The maximum late release occurs from the point where the hands have reached the bottom of the arc, below the left shoulder, and with the wrists still fully cocked.

As the wrists uncock and the forearms begin to roll, the forearms square the clubface up to the ball at impact.

Next, the right arm straightens, giving a downward and outward extension of the clubhead.

After impact the momentum of the club completes the crossover of the forearms.

When the hands reach the bottom of the arc, the release, follow through and finish will follow.

**IMPORTANT:** *It is essential throughout the downswing that the head remains up and that the hip turn leads throughout.*

**DRILLS**  1. From the top, feel you are drawing an arrow from a quiver with your right hand.
2. From the top, imagine you are driving a stake into the ground, opposite the right foot.

## RELEASE POINT

**IMPORTANT:** *Keep the head stationary and the shoulders turning on as vertical a plane as possible.*
*The left wrist remains flat, the right wrist bent and, the feet remain heavy in the ground.*

| START DOWN | NEAR LATE RELEASE | RELEASE POINT | IMPACT |

AFTER IMPACT      CROSSOVER      FOLLOW THROUGH      FINISH

### DRILLS

**1. THE HITCH-HIKER** With the left arm in the ready to be released position (level with the right hip pocket) and with the hand clenched thumb up and left wrist flat, move the butt of your hand smoothly down towards the ball. As the hand reaches the bottom of its arc roll the left forearm completely keeping the back of the left wrist flat. The thumb will completely roll over to face skyward again. Feel the complete unwinding and rewinding of the left forearm.

**2. THE TYRE DRILL** From around waist high, with club fully gripped, aim the butt of the left hand down at the tyre. As the left hip turns into a firm left leg, the clubhead will slap the back centre of the tyre promoting a firm, flat left wrist and bent right wrist.

## FOLLOW THROUGH

The swinging club continues, from the crossover, to drag the arms, shoulders, right hip, right leg and right foot up to the finish. From the crossover, the head is also dragged up and around gradually, to follow the flight of the ball. At this point the balance and weight are predominantly on the left side and the body is in a straight-line position over the front left foot. Shoulders are level.

**IMPORTANT** *Keep the left foot as flat on the ground as possible while the right foot is dragged up to finish on the inside edge of the big toe.*
*Ninety eight percent of the body weight is on the left side.*

AFTER IMPACT      CROSSOVER      FOLLOW THROUGH      FINISH

# WEIGHT DISTRIBUTION AND TRANSFERENCE

In a powerful, dynamic swing, balance and weight transference are critical. Both feet are trying to stay planted in the ground but the body pivot drags the feet up, pushes them down and drags them up again.

**At address** The *weight distribution is 50–50.* The feet are flat and heavy in the ground.

**Takeaway** The left heel is dragged up as the foot rolls to the inside ball of the left foot. Seventy per cent of the weight is on the inside of the right foot.

**Top of backswing** Here the full pivot of the body has turned around the inside of the right foot putting approximately 80% of the weight on the inside of the right foot.

**Start down** To start the downswing the left hip turns into the left side returning the left heel firmly to the ground. The weight starts transferring to the left foot.

**Impact** Ninety-five per cent of the body weight is now on the left side. Note that due to the downward thrust of the swing the pressure against the ground increases, therefore, the effective weight in each foot increases. You feel as if you are sinking into the ground.

**Follow through** Ninety-eight per cent of body weight is on the left foot.

**Cross over** Ninety-eight per cent of body weight is on the left side as the swinging club drags the body through and up.

**Finish** Ninety-eight per cent of body weight is now balanced over the front foot. The left foot is flat on the ground. The 2% of weight on the right foot is concentrated on the inside ball of the right foot.

# HAND ACTION

Correct hand action is critical to produce the uncompensated golf swing. The left wrist must remain flat at all times, after address and before the finish position. The right wrist must remain cupped (bent) at all times to prevent clubhead throwaway.

**BACKSWING** In the backswing, the wrists cock on the plane of the flat left wrist while the forearms roll.

**DOWNSWING** In the downswing, the wrists finally uncock at the late release point and the forearms roll square. In the follow through, maximum uncocking is followed by complete forearm roll and recocking of the wrists.

**IMPACT TO FINISH** The left wrist never cups and remains flat to slightly arched through impact and beyond. The right wrist remaining cupped (or bent) to help produce maximum forearm roll and the free wheeling release.

**ADDRESS** LEFT WRIST VERTICAL, RIGHT WRIST VERTICAL

**IMPACT** LEFT WRIST FLAT, RIGHT WRIST CUPPED

**ADDRESS** ARMS IN NATURAL HANGING POSITION

**IMPACT** WRISTS UNCOCKED

**CORRECT HAND ACTION** *ties the arms into the pivot, bringing the elbows toward each other. The coiling of the hands, arms and shoulders is dependent on the precision of the wrist action. Without it, the arms work independently from the body pivot and timing becomes extremely difficult.*

**TOP OF BACKSWING** LEFT WRIST FLAT CLUB SHAFT ON PLANE AND AIMING AT TARGET. WRISTS FULLY COCKED

**TOP OF BACKSWING**

**WRISTS IN COCKED POSITION** LEFT WRIST FLAT, RIGHT WRIST CUPPED

**FULLY UNCOCKED POSITION**

# BODY PIVOT — HIPS

**ADDRESS** HIP POSITION PARALLEL TO TARGET LINE

Body pivot is the central core of the swing and therefore, the foundation of a free-wheeling uncompensated swing. With body pivot we have two sections of the body to consider — *THE HIP TURN* and *THE SHOULDER TURN*.

It is my preference to consider that the hip turn is the *motor* in the swing and that the shoulders respond to both the hip turn and the hand and arm actions. The shoulder turn is a relatively passive but specific movement.

**HIP TURN** The hips do turn but they have three centres of rotation at different stages in the swing.

**BACKSWING** The hips rotate around the middle of the hips in the backswing (turning in a barrel) giving the feeling of sinking back onto the right hip. The right knee remaining flexed as the weight transfers to the inside ball of the right foot.

**DOWNSWING** To start the downswing, the left hip turns around the right hip as axis, bringing the left heel back flat on the ground. The left leg begins to straighten.

**IMPACT TO FINISH** From a solid braced left leg the right hip now turns around the left hip as axis as I swing to the finish.

**BACKSWING** HIP TURN RIGHT HIP BACK

**DRILL** *Place several golf balls under the outside edge of the right foot to stop swaying backwards.*

START DOWN HIP TURNS LEFT

**IMPACT** LEFT LEG STRAIGHT RIGHT FOOT DRAGGED TO INSIDE BALL OF FOOT

**FINISH** WEIGHT MOSTLY ON LEFT SIDE — HIPS TURNED FULLY LEFT

**ADDRESS** RIGHT SHOULDER
BELOW LEFT, SHOULDERS
PARALLEL TO TARGET LINE

# BODY PIVOT — SHOULDERS

As previously mentioned, the shoulders turn in
response to the hips and the hand and arm action.
They have a very specific function and incorrect
shoulder rotation can be very disruptive.

The shoulders are followers not leaders in the swing
motion, especially at the beginning of the
downswing.

**BACKSWING** In the backswing the shoulders turn
as flat as possible — the left shoulder remains as high
and the right shoulder stays as low as possible.

**DOWNSWING TO FOLLOW THROUGH** In
the start of the downswing the left shoulder resists
the turn of the hips slightly and in the process
moves more up than around. This creates a
downswing shoulder turn that is as upright as
possible.

At impact and to the follow through position (both
arms straight) the shoulders remain parallel to the
target line.

**FOLLOW THROUGH TO FINISH** Once you
have straightened the right arm fully and the
forearms begin to crossover, the arms pull the right
shoulder up and around creating a flat shoulder turn
to the finish.

**TOP BACKSWING** SHOULDER
TURN AS FLAT AS POSSIBLE,
BACKBONE ON SAME INCLINE AS
ADDRESS

**NEARING IMPACT** RIGHT
SHOULDER LOW, LEFT SHOULDER
HIGH

**CROSS OVER POSITION IN FOLLOW
THROUGH** RIGHT SHOULDER
STILL LOW, LEFT SHOULDER HIGH

**FINISH** SHOULDER TURN FROM
CROSSOVER FLATTENS,
DRAGGING HEAD UP AND
FORWARD

# III
# SHOTMAKING AND
# TROUBLE SHOTS

# PUTTING

## THE FOUR BASICS OF GOOD PUTTING

1. Keep the putter face at right angles to the line of the putt at impact.
2. Keep the path of the putter head straight back and straight through.
3. Keep the path of the putter head parallel and low to the ground at impact.
4. Accelerate the stroke at the correct speed at impact.

It has been said that putting is an individual thing. I, like Paul Runyan, believe that this could not be further from the truth.

Putting requires the utmost precision and therefore requires a precise method. There are three basic putting strokes: 1. Wrists only (Billy Casper) 2. Wrists and arms (Ben Crenshaw) 3. Arms only (Jack Nicklaus, Tom Watson, Bob Charles, Paul Runyan, Jane Lock).

Because arms only putting is a one lever stroke, no timing is required. This allows for more precision in contacting the ball squarely and thereby increases your chances of holing more putts.

Sure, there are great putters using wrist only and wrist and arm techniques, but these players rely more heavily on their natural abilities and a steady nerve.

Putting requires a positive attitude, the ability to visualise, plenty of practice and a sound method. The ability to perform well over a long period is the true test of a method's soundness.

RUNYAN GRIP

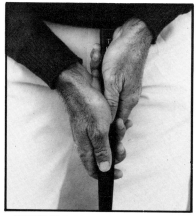

STANDARD PALMS PARALLEL GRIP

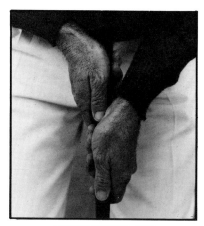

REVERSE HAND GRIP

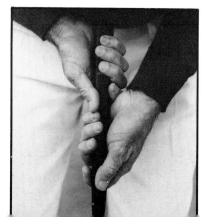

REVERSE RUNYAN

# PUTTING GRIP

1. The grip of the putter lies across the left hand, from the crease above the little finger to the first joint of the forefinger. The palm faces outward.
2. Next, wrap the fingers around the grip and place the pad of the left thumb against the top left quarter of the grip.
3. The putter grip lies predominantly in the fingers. The grip pressure is light.

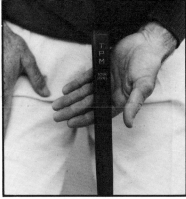

LEFT HAND

# RIGHT HAND

The little finger overlaps with the forefinger of the left hand.

1. The middle two fingers touch the grip at the base of the fingers. The palm faces outward.
2. Wrap the fingers around the grip and place the pad of the right thumb on the top right hand quarter of the grip.
3. A·pressure point can be felt when the crease above the little finger of the right hand presses against the left index finger. The grip is predominantly in the fingers. The grip pressure is light.

The hands are equally opposed with the forearms at approximately 45° to the shaft. This is the neutral position for the hands. The shaft and the forearms are in the same plane of action, parallel to the line of the putt.

LEFT HAND CLOSED

# PUTTING PSYCHOLOGY

1. The worst thing you can do is miss, so don't worry!
2. A smooth, rhythmic, solid hit is your key to a consistent roll.

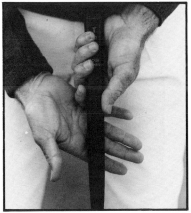

RIGHT HAND POSITION

FINGERNAILS ON TOP OF GRIP

THE BEST PLACE TO ASSEMBLE AND CHECK THE GRIP IS OPPOSITE ELBOW HEIGHT WHEN STANDING UPRIGHT THE FOREARMS AND SHAFT OF PUTTER SAME LEVEL.

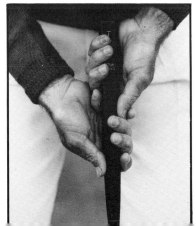

AN IDEAL FEET POSITION TO
CHECK YOUR GRIP AND ARMS.

# STANCE
# AND STROKE

1. Feet are at right angles to the target line. The line along the toes is parallel to the target line. Feet are set a comfortable distance apart for solid balance.
2. Ball position is on the inside edge of left foot.
3. Elbows rest gently against the side of the body, about 45° to the shaft.
4. Shaft and forearms are kept in the same plane of action.
5. Club shaft vertical to ground (*looking front on*).
6. Weight 60% on left side.
7. Eyes are directly over target line. Feet, knees, hips, shoulders, eyes and forearms are parallel to the target line.
8. The posture has two bends: at the hips and at the knees. Bend over close to your work.
9. The stroke is a one lever action with the arms swinging from the shoulder socket. There is no body or wrist action. This produces a straight back and straight through stroke with the putter head staying close to the ground for most of the stroke.
10. A short firm tapping action works best. Imagine you are driving a tack into the back of the ball.
11. Hit the ball half way up.

**IMPORTANT** *The eyes must remain fixed on the back of the ball. (Eyes on the ball but your mind on your hands.)*

ADDRESS POSITION

CHECKING EYES OVER TARGET
LINE AND BEHIND BALL.

PARALLEL STANCE

BACKSTROKE

FOLLOW THROUGH STROKE

# PUTTING DRILLS

**STRAIGHT LINE DRILL** Place a number of balls in a straight line on a level part of the green starting at two feet. Roll the balls over the front edge of the hole in turn, progressively working to longer distances from the hole. This technique develops a feel for distance. Vary the speed with which the ball goes into the hole to develop fine tuning on touch.

The best putters are those that roll the ball to the hole and not too aggressively.

*Dead strength putting is the key.*

STRAIGHT LINE DRILL FOR DISTANCE CONTROL.

PARALLEL RODS FOR PRACTISING.

**CIRCLE DRILL** Place a number of balls in an arc or circle of two foot radius around the hole with some degree of slope. Holing each putt out in turn gives you the variation in borrow and degrees of uphill and downhill. This teaches you to read the slope on the green. Extend the radius as you desire and your depth of feel of slopes will increase.

As you become proficient with reading both distance and slope, move the hole in your imagination to create a straight putt approach.

*(Every putt is a straight putt — the hole just isn't where you think it is.)*

**PARALLEL RODS** Regular use develops muscle memory and positive feedback from holing many putts in a row. The stroke moves straight back and straight through, alignment can be checked and the clubface kept square.

# FAULTS AND CURES

## PULLING OR HOOKING PUTTS

1. Check eyes are not moving and are over the line of the putt.
2. Check feet, shoulders, forearms and eyes are all parallel to the target line.
3. Check clubface is at right angles to the line at address.
4. Check hand position — move top (left) hand further under (to the left).

## PUSHING OR CUTTING PUTTS

**1, 2, 3**, as above.
4. Check hand position — move bottom (right) hand further under (to the right).

CIRCLE DRILL FOR LEARNING BORROW SLOPE CONTROL.

SHORT FIRM STROKE.
ARM ACTION ONLY.

WEIGHT FORWARD AND HAND
AHEAD AT IMPACT.

FOLLOW THROUGH LOW,
PUTTING THE HANDLE IN THE
HOLE.

# CHIP AND RUN

The chip and run shot is no more than a putt with a more lofted club.

Generally, height and spin are to be avoided as much as possible on chip shots. To do this use the least lofted club that will land the ball on the green and still stop near the hole.

There is no need for power in this shot, so the wrist-free putting technique can be applied. The advantages of the simpler wrist-free strokes are that more solid contact, improved accuracy, and easier distance control can be achieved.

**THE STROKE** This is an arms stroke with little wrist movement and a short, firm, tapping action to give minimum motion and firm acceleration. There is little or no body action.

**PRACTICAL DRILLS** Start with a 4 iron from one or two yards off the edge of the green and carry the ball onto a spot within a small circle that is between one and two yards on the green. Note the distance the ball runs on. Do the same with the 5, 6, 7, 8 and 9 irons, wedge and sand iron. This can be repeated at varying distances to develop touch and judgement.

STROKE STRAIGHT BACK,
.PARALLEL STANCE.

EYES STEADY WATCHING BACK
OF BALL. FEET, HIPS, SHOULDERS,
FOREARMS AND EYES SQUARE TO
LINE.

STROKE STRAIGHT THROUGH,
PUTTING HANDLE IN THE HOLE.

THE CLUB GRIP RUNS ACROSS THE LEFT HAND, FROM ABOVE THE LITTLE FINGER TO THE FIRST JOINT OF THE FOREFINGER.

THE FINGERS CLOSE AROUND THE GRIP. THE PAD OF THE LEFT THUMB IS PLACED ON THE TOP LEFT QUARTER OF THE GRIP.

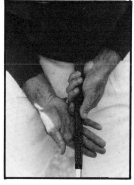

THE RIGHT HAND OVERLAPS THE INDEX FINGER OF THE LEFT HAND SLIGHTLY. THE GRIP TOUCHES THE RIGHT HAND AT THE BASE OF THE FINGER.

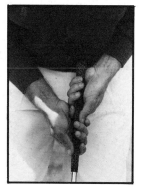

THE RIGHT FINGERS CLOSE AROUND THE GRIP. THE THUMB IS PLACED ON THE TOP RIGHT QUARTER OF THE GRIP. GRIP PRESSURE IS LIGHT.

**THE GRIP** Both hands are placed lower on the grip than normal with the palms facing inward and upward half-way between vertical and horizontal. Hold the club with equally light pressure in both hands and hold the club at address so that only a small fraction of its weight sits on the grass.

**WEIGHT DISTRIBUTION** Lean more on the front foot to bring the base of the neck to the front side of the ball. This allows a pinching action for solid contact.

The butt of the club always points at the left groin.

Move the hands further forward for bad lies so that the downward pinching action becomes more acute.

**THE ARMS** Both forearms are placed at 45° to the shaft in the direction of the target line. The upper arms rest lightly against the rib cage.

**FEET** Both feet are at right angles to the target line. The line across the toes is parallel to the target line.

**POSTURE AND BALL POSITION** Most of the bend is from the hips, with a slight knee flex to get down close to your work. The ball is positioned directly below the eyes. The line across the eyes is parallel to the target line.

The ball is positioned in the middle of the stance, but moved back for poorer lies.

# THE PITCH SHOT

The pitch shot is one that can save or ruin a score more quickly than any other. It is for this reason that the golfer should learn the key factors which lead to consistent and accurate pitching.

The pitch shot generally flies high and has more air time than ground time. It is played when a quick stopping shot is required.

## THE KEY FACTORS

**1. Grip** The standard grip is used. The right hand V formed by the thumb and forefinger must point at the chin. Hands are placed lower on the grip than normal.

**2. Under reaching** The clubhead is held slightly off the ground.

**3. Ball position** For standard pitch shots the ball is placed in the centre of the stance or slightly back of centre.

**4. Address** The feet are closer together than for full shots. The line across the toes is parallel to the target line. Stand tall with a slight bend at the hips and flex at the knees.

HANDS LOWER ON GRIP

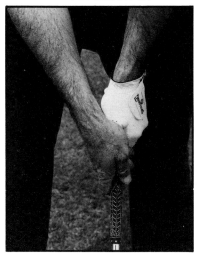

| STANCE | HIP TURN DRAGS THE CLUB AWAY | THE WRISTS ARE HINGING FREELY | FULL WRIST COCK | HIP TURN DRAGS THE CLUB DOWN |

44

**PLANNING** The proper order of procedure is to visualise the shot, to determine where the pitch should drop and how much roll it should have.

Then select the club and attempt the shot that should produce this result. Always favour a straightforward shot and go to a more lofted club only when it is necessary to stop the ball quickly.

**THE STANDARD PINCHED PITCH** This is the safest pitch shot and is the one most often used. The ball is positioned slightly back of centre and the weight favours the front foot.

The ball is trapped between the clubface and the turf on the downswing. This shot produces good back spin but the loft of the club is reduced so the ball flies lower than normal. This shot is useful for less than perfect lies and into the wind.

**STEADY HEAD** Once you have assessed the distance and direction, keep your eyes fixed positively on the back of the ball and watch the divot. Your head must remain absolutely still. It must not dip down.

I hope you have as much success with this technique as I have and remember that confidence grows with practice.

**IMPORTANT** The pitch shot is a miniature full swing. The hip turn leads the club back and through around a steady centre. Feel you control distance with your lower body and less with your hands. The shorter the pitch the more active the hip turn. *Good pitch shot players stay up and throw the clubhead down, bad pitch shot players do the opposite.*

LATE RELEASE POSITION     IMPACT FIRM LEFT SIDE     FOLLOW THROUGH     REVERSE ROLL     FINISH

45

# THE CUT PITCH

To increase height and stopping ability, an open clubface will give more loft and cut spin. However, when executing this shot, you must aim left to allow for the slicing action. And don't forget to hit down firmly.

**GRIP PRESSURE** On all cut pitch shots the grip pressure is firmer than a full shot as you do not want forearm roll through the ball. The clubface must remain open at all times throughout the swing.

**WEIGHT DISTRIBUTION** The weight favours the left foot and remains there throughout the swing.

| **OPEN STANCE** | **TOP OF BACKSWING** TOE OF CLUB POINTS TO THE SKY | **START DOWN** HIP TURNS LEFT, DRAGS CLUB DOWN. | CLUB HEAD MOVING ACROSS THE LINE. | **FINISH** TOE OF CLUB DOES NOT CROSS OVER. CLUBFACE OPEN. |

At the completion of the swing the toe of the clubface and the forearms have not crossed over. A reverse roll of the forearms has occured which has kept the clubface open throughout the swing.

The weight is firmly on the left side, and the body faces the target.

# THE PITCH AND RUN

This shot is most effective when you have plenty of green between you and the hole or if you have a bank to go over. The pitch and run flies lower and faster and has less backspin than the pitch shot. In your pre-shot preparation it is important to visualise rolling the ball over the surface and towards the hole.

### ADDRESS
Use a slightly closed stance, aim the clubface at the target and play the ball from the centre of the stance or slightly back of centre.

**HAND ACTION** Let the hip turn roll the clubface back and through. In the follow through the right forearm fully crosses over the left.

ADDRESS

TAKEAWAY

TOP OF BACKSWING

START DOWN

IMPACT

FOLLOW THROUGH
ROLL OVER

MOVING TO FINISH

FINISH

# LOB SHOT

When the lie is extremely good and a high, quick-stopping shot is required, the lob shot is the one to play. For this shot the ball is positioned further towards the front foot. The ball is struck at the bottom of the swing or even slightly on the upswing.

The effective loft on the club is at a maximum at impact. To get maximum height and backspin open the clubface.

**GRIP PRESSURE** On lob shots the grip pressure is slightly less than with the cut shot.

**WEIGHT DISTRIBUTION** The weight in the feet is more evenly distributed.

**IMPORTANT** *Visualise lifting the ball steeply and develop a positive feel for the shot in your pre-shot preparation.*

# THE PINCH SHOT

When the lie is less than perfect, you are playing into the wind, or the pin is cut well back in the green, the pinched pitch is the percentage shot.

1. Play the ball nearer the right foot with a square to slightly open stance.
2. Place more weight on the left side and lean more towards the target.
3. Hold the clubhead slightly off the ground.
4. Lead back and through with the hip turn.
5. Use *firm wrists* and a steep backswing arc.
6. Stay up through the downswing.

# STANDARD PITCH — 50 YARDS

Front on view of 50 yard pitch, the standard pinch shot with a sand iron. The sand iron gives height and stopping power for close in pitch shots.

Rear view of 50 yard pitch. Note that the backswing is long enough for a smooth accelerating stroke into the ball.

# DRAWS AND FADES

The draw and fade shots are required as part of every good golfers game.

You need to shape your shots not only to manoeuvre the ball around trouble, but also to help straighten shots into crosswinds.

## THE DRAW SHOT

For right handed golfers a draw or hook shot starts right of target and curves to the left.

**Stance** Aim to the right of the target and move the ball slightly more forward in the stance.

**Clubface** Aim the clubface at the target, or left of target for greater curve.

**Grip** *Relax* the tension in your hands and forearms to promote a more oily wrist action.

**Swing** Use a standard full swing and focus on allowing your swing path to parallel your feet line. The ball will start to the right and curve left.

ALIGNMENT AND SWING PATH
RIGHT OF TARGET

USE A NEUTRAL HAND POSITION
AND CLOSED CLUBFACE

**IMPORTANT** *Draw and hook shots travel lower and further than straight shots. Allow for this by selecting less club than you would use if hitting a straight shot.*

# THE FADE SHOT

For the right handed golfer a fade or slice shot starts to the left of target and curves to the right.

**Stance** Aim to the left of the target and move the ball slightly more back in your stance.

**Clubface** Aim the clubface at the target, or right of target for greater curve.

**Grip** *Firm up* your hands to restrict wrist action and forearm roll.

**Swing** Use a standard full swing and focus on allowing your swing path to parallel your feet line. The ball will start to the left and curve right.

ALIGNMENT AND SWING PATH
LEFT OF TARGET

USE AN OPEN CLUBFACE

**IMPORTANT** *Fade and slice shots travel higher and shorter than straight shots. Allow for this by selecting more club than you would use if hitting a straight shot.*

# THE HIGH SHOT

The high shot is played to clear objects in front of you or when a soft-landing shot to a firm green is required.

1. Position the ball forward in your stance.
2. Stand slightly further away from the ball than on normal shots and picture sweeping the ball.
3. Rest the club lightly on the ground.
4. Weight favours the back foot slightly.
5. Use a standard full swing.

**IMPORTANT** *You must keep a steady centre.*

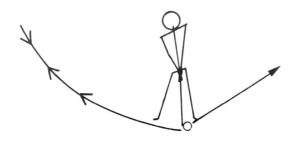

ANGLES OF ATTACK AND BALL FLIGHT

# THE LOW SHOT

The low shot is useful on windy days and to keep the ball under obstacles such as trees.

**1.** Position the ball back in your stance.
**2.** Stand taller and slightly closer to the ball than on normal shots.
**3.** Rest the club lightly on the ground.
**4.** Lean slightly forward with the weight more on the front foot.
**5.** The swing action is a punch shot routine where you hit down on the shot with a shortened follow-through.

**IMPORTANT** *The weight stays on the left side while the hip turn leads the swing back and through.*

ANGLES OF ATTACK AND BALL FLIGHT

# THE PUNCH SHOT

With little or no follow through you can still punch the shot a considerable distance.

**1.** Move the ball well back in your stance.
**2.** Lean forward towards the left foot.
**3.** Push your hands well forward and hood the clubface.
**4.** Make a normal swing, making sure you hit down steeply and swing firmly.
**5.** When the clubhead hits the ball and then the ground it will stop abruptly.

**IMPORTANT** *As this shot could cause serious damage to your hands and arms, always play the shot well within your maximum power.*

# THE BOB CHARLES SHOT

**HITTING LEFT HANDED** When confronted with the ball close to a tree or other obstacle and a right handed swing is impossible, change to a left handed position.

**1.** Preferably choose a 7, 8, 9 or wedge and turn the clubhead over.
**2.** Take a left hander's stance and grip, and keep the toe slightly off the ground.
**3.** Make a smooth easy swing around a quiet, steady centre. Don't overswing. A solid hit will get you surprising distance.

# THE BOBBY CLAMPETT SHOT

**HITTING OFF YOUR KNEES** A knee level stance will flatten and lower your swing considerably.

1. From a balanced, relaxed address position on your knees, make predominantly an arms and wrist swing around a quiet steady centre.
2. Open the clubface at address, as there will be a tendency to hook the shot.
3. As a great deal of your power is transferred through your arms and hands, good distance can be achieved from this shot with practice.

To prove that leg action was not as important as some professionals had emphasised, Bobby Clampett hit a driver off his knees over 200 metres in the U.S. open. At the time he was heading for an early exit after the 36-hole cut.

# BALL BELOW FEET

When the ball is below your feet make the following adjustments to your address and then swing normally.

**1. Posture** Bend over more from the hips and make sure your balance is good.

**2. Close clubface** slightly as the ball will tend to slice from this hanging lie.

**3. Swing** smoothly around a quiet, steady centre, being careful to retain balance. Your swing will be slightly more upright because of the greater bend in your posture, so use one more club than normal (less lofted).

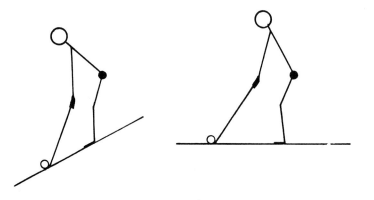

**IMPORTANT** *Stay down on the shot as long as possible.*

# BALL ABOVE FEET

When the ball is above your feet make the following adjustments to your address and then swing normally.

**1. Posture** Stand slightly more upright and rest the club on the ground lightly behind the ball. Keep your balance on the balls of your feet.

**2. Open** the clubface slightly as the ball will tend to hook when it is above your feet.

**3. Swing** smoothly around a steady, quiet centre. Pay attention to swinging in balance. Your swing will be slightly flattened because of your upright posture. You will tend to get slightly more distance so grip down on the grip slightly. This also promotes solid contact and control.

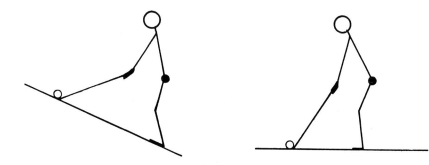

**IMPORTANT** *Keep your head up at the address position otherwise there is a tendency to hit the ball fat.*

# DOWNHILL LIE

With the downhill lie there is a tendency to push or slice the shot and hit the ball lower.

1. To avoid hitting the ground behind the ball, move the ball back in the stance slightly and lean towards the front foot.
2. Take one club less than normal (more lofted).
3. Close the clubface slightly to lessen the push or slice.
4. Swing smoothly around a quiet, steady centre and hit down and out to promote solid contact.

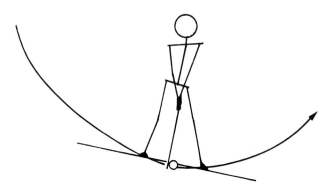

# UPHILL LIE

With the uphill lie there is a tendency to pull or hook the shot and hit the ball higher. To correct this do the following:

1. Marry your posture to the slope by leaning back slightly. Keep your backbone perpendicular to the slope.
2. Play the ball slightly more forward.
3. Take one more club than normal.
4. Open the clubface slightly and grip down the shaft slightly.
5. Swing smoothly around a quiet, steady centre and swing up the slope.

# GREENSIDE BUNKERS

Greenside bunkers require a special technique to allow you to swing positively without over shooting the target. The sand iron is designed especially for these shots. Sand irons have between 55° and 60° loft and a trailing edge that is lower than the leading edge which produces a bounce effect off the sand.

## BUNKER PLAY PRINCIPLES

1. Establish a firm stance by burying your feet in the sand.
2. Place 60% of your weight on your left foot.
3. Position the ball off the instep of the left foot.
4. Use a slightly open stance. The shorter the shot the more open the stance.
5. Position your hands down the grip for more control. Keep the clubface slightly open and the right hand V pointing up at the chin.
6. Standing tall enough and far enough away from the ball with the arms fully stretched, hold the club one to two inches above the spot you wish to hit, one inch behind the ball.
7. Bend the left wrist inward at address to establish maximum loft on the sand iron and to enable the trailing edge of the sand iron to hit the sand first, creating the bounce effect off the sand.

8. To control the distance of the shot, change the angle of the backswing arc. Use a steep angle for short shots and a shallow angle for longer shots. For maximum stop on very short shots use a very open stance and clubface and a steep angle of attack. Use firm wrists throughout.

9. The follow through is the product of the clubhead bouncing off the sand and will automatically occur if the left wrist remains cupped.

10. Always use the hips to swing the club back and through. Wrist action should be kept to a minimum. Always have a full pivot through the ball and finish in balance.

11. Use reverse roll of the forearms to promote softer higher flying shots.

    *Practice is required to develop the feel for this shot. Head must remain steady to give a consistent strike. STAY UP AND HIT DOWN.*

**Wet or hard sand** Make the backswing steeper and hit more downward. You will get more backspin out of this shot.

**Dry soft sand** Make the backswing shallower, have the weight more even and use of a more cutting action to lift the ball out.

*BUNKERS ARE HAZARDS AND YOU MUST NOT GROUND YOUR CLUB AT ANY TIME BEFORE IMPACT.*

# THE BURIED LIE

It is important to utilize the rebound principle to blast the ball from the sand.

1. Square up stance and clubface to minimise bounce effect. Perhaps use the wedge to get under the ball.
2. Establish a firm stance with up to 70% of your weight on the left foot.
3. Use the hip turn and arm lift to establish a steep angle on the backswing.
4. Aim to hit one inch behind the ball, burying the clubhead in the sand below the ball. No need to follow through.

**IMPORTANT** *With buried lies there is little or no backspin produced so allow for extra run in your pre-shot planning.*

# THE UPHILL LIE

With uphill bunker shots the ball will fly higher and stop quicker. Therefore a shallower angle of attack is required to project the ball to the hole than if the ball were lying on a flat surface of the same distance.

Apply standard *BUNKER PRINCIPLES* with the following adjustments:

1. Lean back more over the right foot — marrying your stance to the slope.
2. Use a square stance as opposed to the slightly open stance of the normal bunker shot.
3. Aim to hit one to two inches behind the ball with a shallow angle of attack.

# THE DOWNHILL LIE

With downhill bunker shots the ball will fly lower and run more, therefore a steeper angle of attack is required to project the ball to the hole.

Apply standard *BUNKER PRINCIPLES* with the following adjustments.

1. Lean forward more over the left foot — marrying your stance to the slope.
2. Use a slightly more open stance and more open club face.
3. Aim to hit one to two inches behind the ball with a steeper angle of attack and chase the clubhead down the slope.

# FAIRWAY BUNKERS

RIGHT FOOT ANGLED INTO THE
SAND BOTH FEET SECURELY
PLANTED IN THE SAND

**ADDRESS** BALL POSITION
SLIGHTLY BACK OF CENTRE

**TOP OF BACKSWING** MORE
COMPACT THAN FULL SWING

In a fairway bunker, the objective changes. Here, we are seeking distance and clean contact. Our first aim is to clear the bunker lip, therefore choose enough club to do so with ease.

**STANCE** Stand far enough away and erect enough to have the clubhead above and behind the ball. Place the ball in the centre of the stance or back of centre with the weight favouring the front foot. Secure your feet solidly in the sand with the right instep more deeply set in the sand to act as a solid axis for the swing and to help promote a slightly steeper angle of attack. Hood the clubface slightly.

**THE SWING** The swing should be about three quarter length. Turn around a quiet, steady centre, allowing the hips to lead back and through in a positive rotation. Always swing through to balance.

**ETIQUETTE** Always smooth out your foot marks when leaving the bunker.

**IMPORTANT** *Even though you turn around the inside of the right foot as axis there is little or no weight transfer in the backswing — 50% of your weight remains on your left side.*

**NEARING IMPACT**
LEFT HIP CLEAR, LEFT LEG
STRAIGHT

**FOLLOW THROUGH**
HITTING PAST THE CHIN

**FINISH**
SIMILAR TO BACKSWING;
COMPACT, FEET FIRMLY
PLANTED, SHOULDERS LEVEL,
FINISH IN BALANCE OVER FRONT
FOOT.

# IV
# STRATEGY AND
# <u>PREPARATION</u>

# HOW TO WARM UP
# FOR A ROUND OF GOLF

To play to your best in a competition pre-game preparation is very important.
An effective warm up practice before the game, combined with a healthy, relaxed
state of mind, will ensure you are giving yourself every chance to perform well.

## FULL WARM UP PROGRAMME

Arrive at the course one hour before your tee time. Go to the practice putting
green and start with three-foot putts on a flat section of the green. Hit between
10 and 20 putts from this distance before progressing to two yards, three yards,
out to 10 yards.

● Following approximately 15 minutes of putting practice move out to chip and
run shots from around the edge of the green. Try various clubs from sand iron
to 5 iron.

● Allow 30 minutes to hit full shots on the practice fairway and if possible
practice a few bunker shots. Start with your short irons (eg. wedge or 9 iron)
and hit some half and three-quarter shots before starting on the full swing.

● It is better to hit a few shots with as many clubs as possible rather than hit a
lot of shots with one club.

● Warming up for a round of golf is different from practising to improve your
technique so keep your swing keys to a minimum and focus on balance, rhythm,
and tempo. Solid contact to a specific target is your aim here.

If you have time it is best to allocate 15–30 minutes a day to stretching exercises
so that your muscles will be ready to perform without injury.

Not all golfers will have adequate time to apply the best approach to play so I
have included some alternatives.

**THE FIVE MINUTE PLAN** Start with five one-foot putts progressing to
two, three, four and five feet. Continue with five putts from five and 10 yards.
Move to the edge of the green and hit five chip and run shots from 10 and 15
yards. Finish with five full practice swings with a driver plus three deep breaths
before teeing up.

**THE 15 MINUTE PLAN** The five minute plan plus 20 range balls with
wedge, 7 iron, 4 iron, and 3 wood or driver or 20 shots into the practice net.

**THE 30 MINUTE PLAN** The 15 minute plan plus bunker and pitching
practice for 10 minutes, plus 3–5 minutes relaxing before you hit off.

# SELECTING THE CORRECT SHOT

The critical time for every golfer occurs at the very beginning of every shot . . . the time involved in planning and getting settled over the ball. The first things to do in planning the shot are:

## 1. CHECK THE LIE

**Lying clearly on flat ground** Set up normally, parallel to target.

**Uphill lie** Aim slightly right (closed stance) as your tendency will be to draw the ball slightly. FIT yourself to the slope by leaning back toward the right side to avoid too deep a divot.

**Downhill lie** Aim slightly left (open stance) as your tendency will be to push or fade the ball slightly. LEAN left to fit yourself to the slope to avoid hitting behind the ball or hitting thin.

**Ball above feet** Stand more erect and aim slightly to the right (closed stance) to allow for draw caused by slope and stance — or aim straight (square stance) and open clubface slightly.

**Ball below feet** Bend over more from waist. Aim slightly to the left (open stance) to allow for fade caused by slope or stance — or aim straight (square stance) and close clubhead slightly.

**In a depression or divot** Take a more lofted club, play the ball back more in the stance and hood the clubface by leaning slightly more on the left side with the hands ahead of the ball. This stance promotes a more downward swing arc and helps avoid striking the ground behind the ball.

**In wet or long grass** Little spin can be imparted so allow for the ball to fly further.

## 2. CHECK THE GREEN LEVEL
If the green is above you the shot will play longer, if below you the shot will play shorter.

## 3. CHECK THE WIND
In crosswinds you will control the shot better and stop the ball quicker by curving the shot against the wind. In doing so you will need slightly more club.

If you are not confident enough to curve the ball so that it holds against the wind, hit the ball square and aim to allow for the wind to drift the ball back to target. The ball will roll more on landing so allow for this in your club selection.

**Head wind** Take more club and grip down the club. Swing slower than normal — it is important to hit easy into the wind.

**Down wind** The ball will carry and roll further, therefore, take less club.

## 4. CHECK THE DISTANCE
With a measurement to the flag and consideration of the above it is now possible to select the right club.

**IMPORTANT** *After taking all the above into account, you must make a positive decision, select the club, flow into the pre-shot routine and focus on the target.*

# THE PRE SHOT ROUTINE

To focus clearly on playing the shot at hand, I have adopted a routine that allows for (a) correct shot selection (b) focusing of concentration and (c) a series of motions that will lead the golfer into a consistently smooth, unhurried swing.

**Photo 1** At the bag. The bag is placed three to four paces off the target line as I plan my shot.
(a) Select a target area that will give the easiest next shot
(b) Calculate distance to target
(c) Is the target uphill or downhill?
(d) Is the lie, flat, below feet, above feet, uphill or downhill, good or bad and is the grass thick and wet?
(e) Assess wind direction and strength
(f) Finally select club.
My lead in procedure now follows as one. I move three to four paces behind the ball with the ball between me and the target. At this point I visualise the shot I have to make. I have a practice swing to assist my feel for the shot.

**Photo 2** Next, I step behind the ball and pick a spot within one to four paces in front of the ball as my intermediate target.

Following one or two deep slow breaths, I move easily to the ball and with the body to the side of the target line and approximately 45° open to the target, I place the clubhead centrally behind the ball with its bottom edge facing at right angles to the target line.

**Photo 3** I aim the clubface in line with the spot. I am well bent over from the hips, my arms hang clear of the body.

**Photo 4** Next I move the left foot into position for ball placement — it varies from between left heel and the middle of the stance, depending on the club being used.

**Photo 5** From here the right foot is moved into position approximately shoulder width apart from the left foot for balance. For a straight shot the line across the heels is parallel.

**Photo 6** As you make the fine tuning adjustments of the feet to be the correct distance from the ball and aimed correctly, the waggle gives the hands their programming for the coming swing.

**Photo 7** Following the waggle, the clubhead is set momentarily behind the ball. At this stage a slight forward turn of the hips moves the hands against the shaft creating the forward press.

**Photo 8** From the forward press the hips recoil smoothly into the backswing turn and in the process the club is dragged into the backswing takeaway. From here the swing is automatic.

1. AT THE BAG

2. LINING UP TO THE TARGET

3. AIMING THE CLUBFACE. BODY HALF OPEN AND BEHIND THE BALL

4. LEFT FOOT POSITIONING

5. RIGHT FOOT POSITIONING FOR BALANCE

6. WAGGLE

7. FORWARD PRESS

8. TAKEAWAY

# THE 15TH CLUB —
## THE MENTAL APPROACH

It has been said that golf is 90% mental and that without good concentration, temperament and a realistic game plan, golf remains a frustrating form of exertion.

In the preceeding lessons I have presented the mechanics of the golf swing from putting through to the full swing.

The aim of my writing is to present to the keen golfer a total package that he or she can transfer to the golf course and feel that with increased application their game can only improve.

However, the mechanics are only a part of the foundation upon which a solid golf game is built. Now I am going to present a second level in the building of your golf abilities.

I believe any instruction must be part of a consistent system to be of any permanent benefit. A well taught golfer rarely breaks down and rarely goes off his or her game completely.

Good golf is played at a reflex action level of muscle memory and any clear division between the mental and physical functions is simply artificial and solely for the purpose of learning.

Only when the pupil is willing and prepared to work at the game on a long term policy and to disregard any immediate results as a measure of their ability can any long lasting progress be achieved.

Now that I have established the game rules for improvement, let me give you something that you can sink your teeth into.

**1. The swing is one and indivisible** from waggle to finish. By constant repetition of the correct action, a comfortable and reliable feel can be developed. You will feel "in the grove" of the correct swing.

Of course, the comfortable, reliable, right feel is not a thing that comes all at once. The more often the same succession of movements can be repeated, the clearer the memory will be — muscular memory will always be more powerful than the application of knowledge and thought.

Without the feeling for the correct swing motion, a consistent and improving golf game cannot be realised.

**2. Play within your limitations.** This area of mental control requires an honest and realistic assessment of your own ability. Your level can be raised but don't try to do so during competition or you will experience more failure than success.

You will find that if you lower your expectations and aim for positions easily within your range, in both distance and direction, the pressure will diminish and the magic of effortless power will be attained.

You must have a realistic game plan for every hole and discipline yourself to stick to it unless conditions dictate otherwise.

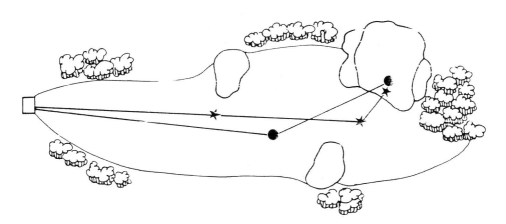

400 METRES.

A LOW MARKER AND HIGH MARKER PLAY THE SAME HOLE.

**3. Don't think in terms of score.** The score is the product of all your shots. You must think of each shot as a game and only take note of the number of shots at the completion of each hole and then start afresh. The time to be a mathematician is at the end of the round. Correct concentration can only be attained when the score is disregarded.

**4. Don't involve yourself in another player's game.** This applies to social golf as well as championship matches.

It is impossible to control what the other player thinks or does. Trying to do so will only distract yourself from what you should be "feeling" i.e. your next shot.

**5. Enjoy your golf.** It is frustrating to play poorly or hit a poor shot, but remember that even the best golfers in the world only hit a few shots each round the way they plan them.

Golf is a game of misses and your attitude is very important if you wish to play near your potential. Any time you see someone get annoyed with their golf you witness golfing immaturity.

Surely it is the challenge of the game played in ideal surroundings with people of similar ideals that makes golf enjoyable.

# MATCHPLAY

Many golfers say that golf is 99% mental and that the difference between golfers is some intangible asset which mysteriously separates them. I am more of a realist and I believe that if a solid basic foundation is established much can be achieved both at the mechanical and mental levels. Therefore we can all improve our matchplay ability.

In matchplay you must stay within your own comfortable limits. It is a trap to try to keep up with a long hitter or try to hit closer to the hole if your opponent has hit a good approach. Remember that the hole is not over until the last putt has been holed.

To be good at matchplay treat both matchplay and strokeplay the same. Play one shot at a time, hit solidly to position, play percentage golf and add the score up only when the game is over. On the putting green hit putts to roll one foot past the hole. Do not give any putts and do not expect to be given any yourself.

Remember that good sportsmanship is also a part of a good match player's make up. Do not plan to put off your opponents and do not take any notice of any of their tactics.

Some days you will do all the right things and still be beaten, but, over the long term, I am sure that the above will help you do your best more often.

# GOLF VIDEO REPLAY

As an instructor I could not teach effectively without the use of a video. Golf is a game that is very much played through the senses of feel and visualization.

A golfer's self image is quite often well removed from the real image and it is only when both self image and the real image are aligned that true learning and improvement can take place. Video gives the student the real image.

To use a video effectively there are three very effective angles:

**1. Front on** From here the student and instructor can see a) the ball position at address, b) head movement, c) body pivot, d) weight transfer.

**2. Down the line** From this position you see a) posture, b) distance from the ball at address, c) swing path, d) right elbow position at top.

**3. Rear** From here you see a) pivot, b) weight transfer, c) right elbow position in back swing, d) left elbow position in follow through, e) arm at top of back swing.

After studying your swing on video replay several times at normal speed, use slow motion, then freeze frame. You need to slow the swing down to fully absorb what your swing is doing. I advise at least 10 reviews before passing judgement. With qualified assistance you can then set about rebuilding the weakest areas while retaining your strong points. It is important to realise your strong points and note the similarities in your swing compared to the orthodox swing.

Only work on one fundamental change at a time and allow time for its integration into your overall swing.

# THE BASEBALL DRILL

The baseball drill highlights a number of important moves: HAND AND ARM ACTION plus the co-ordination of hand and arm action with body pivot. The aim is to swing the club around a steady centre with the club shaft remaining on a horizontal plane.

**Photo 1** First stand erect with the club shaft horizontal and hands opposite chest height. Turn the hip slightly to start the backward motion.

**Photo 2** Allow the left forearm to roll so that the back of the left hand faces up. The wrists are beginning to cock.

**Photo 3** Here, the full wrist cock and clubhead motion has dragged the shoulders further around.

The backswing is a winding up of the power. The right elbow has been fully compressed and the left arm is wound across the chest. The shoulders are wound against the hips. The hips are wound against the feet.

**Photo 4** The swing is led by the hips unwinding first. The hip turn lead drags the club forward, uncocking the wrists. The forearms begin to roll back squaring the clubface opposite the impact position.

**Photo 5** Here, the forearms have crossed over and the left elbow is bending. The back of the left hand is facing down to the ground and the left wrist is flat. The right arm is extended.

**Photo 6** The full club and arm swing plus the hip turn has pulled the shoulders fully through, moving the head smoothly and naturally to the finish position. The wrists have re-cocked and the forearms rolled over.

# THE TYRE DRILL

By swinging easily around a steady centre and aiming to hit solidly the back centre of the tyre, you develop the sense of pouring your power into the impact area. You get the feeling of the flat left wrist, bent right wrist and the squaring up of the clubface at impact.

**IMPORTANT**  *Do not swing too hard. If you overdo this exercise you will damage your hands, wrists and elbows.*

ADDRESS TYRE CENTRE AS ABOVE

BELOW SHOULDER LEVEL BACKSWING

APPROACHING IMPACT

IMPACT — FLAT LEFT WRIST BENT RIGHT WRIST

**SINGLE HANDED TYRE DRILL** Doing this exercise with the left arm improves the strength in the grip and arm and promotes a flat left wrist and forearm roll. Doing this exercise right handed develops the bending of the right elbow in the backswing and the bent right wrist throughout the swing.

**IMPORTANT:** *When doing the one armed drill, swing the arm and club back and through by leading with the pivot.*

# THE DOWN THE TARGET LINE DRILL

**Address position** Use a piece of timber approximately one yard in length. Set up with one end just forward of centre in the stance and place the clubhead squarely against the wood.

**Impact position** Move the hips into the impact position. In the process the right shoulder moves down and the left shoulder up, but both remain parallel to the target line. Move the hands forward, keeping the left wrist flat and pointing at the target and the right wrist bent.

**Follow-through position** Turn the hips to the maximum follow-through position and extend the right arm. In the process push the timber approximately one foot down the line, keeping the clubhead firmly against the timber.

By taking up a new address position you can repeat the process. After several repetitions the timber should have moved forward in a straight line towards the target.

This drill emphasizes the important role that body pivot plays in levering the arms down and out and bringing the body and arms into closer unison.

# PITCHING TO A TARGET

Start with as short a distance as three yards and work back from the pitching target. Set up square to slightly open.

Experiment with (a) different swing lengths and speeds of swing to the same target
(b) degree of openness of stance and clubface
(c) ball position forward and back
(d) degree of closeness to the ball.

By practising to a target you will soon develop the necessary feel for a variety of pitch shots — high and low, slow and fast, stopping, and pitch and run.

# V
# SWING ANALYSIS

# MIKE CLAYTON

Mike Clayton is one of Australia's most talented shot makers. He has great feel for shaping shots and is a particularly good wind player. He was brought up on Melbourne's world famous sand belt courses and loves playing on courses that offer the greatest challenge to his all-round game.

He has been Australian Amateur champion and since turning professional has won the Victorian Open and Tasmanian Open.

His swing is now first rate, although this was not always the case when he first started on tour. As an amateur he had been coached along the Nicklaus lines of "reach for the sky" with as wide an arc as possible. This produced a flying right elbow of which there still remains a slight trace. He is improving it all the time and I have been pleased to assist with these swing changes over the past few years.

Unfortunately Michael is still a perfectionist and he cannot accept less than his best easily. For this reason he has had a temperament problem to date which has lowered his performance record.

I have great confidence that he will overcome this weakness with maturity. His best is still to come.

**At address** A good posture for a man of 187cms (6'2"). His arms are hanging freely. His back is relatively straight and his knees slightly flexed. He is set up parallel to his target line. Balance even in his feet.

**Takeaway** A one piece takeaway where the shoulders, arms, hands and club are moved passively back through a slight hip turn. The clubhead stays outside the hands until the club shaft parallels the ground and the target line. The right knee remains flexed. The head is steady.

| AT ADDRESS | TAKEAWAY | AROUND WAIST HIGH | TOP | STARTING DOWN |

**Around waist high** Wrists well cocked, right elbow bent and left arm straight. The right knee remains flexed while the left knee bends in behind the ball in response to the hip turn.

**Top** Note the knee action. The right knee remains flexed and the left knee is well moved by the hip turn. The left arm is straight. The right elbow points down but not as much as it should. The left wrist is flat. The wrists are fully cocked.

**Starting down** The left hip turns into the left heel dragging the left knee back and pulling the hand in a straight line towards the ball. Note the shaft angle as the right elbow returns close to the side. Both feet are flat on the ground as Mike approaches a hitting position. The head remains stationary.

**Late release** Here Michael's wrists are commencing to uncock. The right elbow is bent and deep in close to the body. The hands are low as the left arm is fully extended down. The shoulders are closed. The hips are open as they unwind against the left foot and leg. The right heel is being dragged out of the ground by this energetic hip action. The head is steady.

**Follow through** Head and back are steady. The hips are cleared. The shoulders are close to parallel to the target line. The right side is moving well below the left through impact. The right arm is now fully extended.

**Crossover** The right arm is dragging the right shoulder up and around. The head is moving with the shoulder pivot. The hips are well turned. The right foot is being dragged out of the ground.

**Approaching finish** The arm swing is turning the shoulders flat and the head keeps moving up and around. The right foot is well up now. The hip turn nearing a full turn to the left.

**Finish** Mike has fully unwound through the ball. Note the bent left elbow and good balance.

LATE RELEASE      FOLLOW THROUGH      CROSSOVER      APPROACHING FINISH      FINISH

# MIKE CLAYTON

**Stance** Note the width of Michael's stance. The ball position is slightly forward of centre. The left shoulder is high, the right shoulder low.

**Takeaway** The clubface is appearing to open gradually but this is an illusion. It is the turn of the body and not the hands that alters the direction in which the clubface points. The head remains steady. Michael is turning around his right foot as axis.

**Around waist high** Note the extension of Michael's left arm. The head remains stationary. The shoulders are well turned on a flat plane. The weight remains solidly on the inside of the right foot. The backbone is on the same tilt as at address. Note the bent left knee.

**Near top** Note the straight left arm. The head is steady. The shoulders have been coiled around that steady centre. The right knee is stationary. The left knee has been moved in behind the ball. The backbone tilt remains constant. A full coil. The wrists are fully cocked. Dynamic balance around the right leg as axis.

**Start down** Note the spread of the knees as the left hip drags the left knee forward and back. The head is steady. The left arm straight. The right elbow sinks towards the side. The hands are wide and you get the impression of Mike dragging the club down and forward toward impact.

STANCE          TAKEAWAY          AROUND WAIST HIGH          NEAR TOP          START DOWN

**Approaching late release** Here the wrists are still cocked as the hands approach the low point. The hips are clearing as the shoulders are being dragged back towards square. The right elbow is low and close into the right side. The head is steady.

**Near impact** The head is steady. Both feet are heavy in the ground. The left side is firm. The hands are slightly ahead of the ball. The left shoulder is high, the right shoulder low. The left arm is straight, the right elbow slightly bent. Most weight is now on Michael's left side.

**Follow through** Head steady (Michael has hit past his chin). The left side is firm. The hips have turned well through the ball. The shoulders are parallel to the target line. The left shoulder is high, his right shoulder low. Both arms are straight. Left wrist is still flat.

**Crossover** Here the arm swing has started to pull Mike's head up and around. The shoulders are turning more left. The right arm is straight and the left elbow is beginning to bend. The left side is firm with the left leg straight. The forearms are crossing over. The right foot is being dragged out of the ground.

**Towards finish** The arm swing has pulled Mike's head up and around further. The right foot has been dragged up with most of the weight now on the left side. The right arm is still straight. The shoulder turn has flattened considerably.

**Finish** Full release. Full pivot. Full weight transfer. Good balance. The club is still firmly gripped in his hands.

APPROACHING LATE RELEASE    NEAR IMPACT    FOLLOW THROUGH    CROSSOVER    TOWARDS FINISH    FINISH

# OSSIE MOORE

Ossie Moore is one of Australia's best strikers of the golf ball. He is a quiet achiever and, although confident in himself, he needs to stretch his ambitions if he is to realize his full potential. He is one of the more studious players and doesn't make changes in his game without careful consideration.

If he has weaknesses it would be in the pitching area, but he has been working hard in this area. His full swing is nearly copy book and his rhythm and temper are worth capturing when he is playing well. If I were to offer any criticism it would be to suggest that his stance could be a little wider and his knee bend a little less at address. This would give him a firmer foundation to swing from.

Ossie is one of my model swingers and a sportsman of whom Australia can be proud.

**Address** A relaxed, balanced position, parallel to the target line with arms hanging freely. Ossie's posture has a little too much knee bend which leads to some lateral slide in the downswing at times.

**Takeaway** A smooth passive start up where hips, shoulders, arms, hands and club move away together. The hip and leg muscles allow for this passive relaxed movement.

**Waist high** Note the extent of the hip turn has moved the left knee to point out and behind the ball. The wrists are hinging freely and the right elbow is bending. The left arm is stretching.

| ADDRESS | TAKEAWAY | WAIST HIGH | AT THE TOP | START DOWN |

**At the top** A full wind up. The left arm is straight and right elbow pointing down. The wrists are fully cocked. The hip turn and shoulder turn are fully wound around a steady centre. Note the flexed right knee.

**Start down** Ossie has started to transfer his weight back to his left heel. The left shoulder resists, allowing the hands to start to drag the club down towards the late release position.

**The sit position** As the hips turn into the left heel the hands move deeper toward the ball, dragging the club downward. This gives the appearance that Ossie is sitting down. Note the deepness of the right elbow.

**Approaching late release** The hips have cleared, the hands are near the bottom of their arc. The wrists are fully cocked with the shoulders parallel to the target line.

**Follow through** Both arms have extended and the shoulders are beginning to unwind past the chin. Note the right heel is being dragged off the ground.

**The crossover** Note that the club has been swung up and around to the inside. The hand has been moved up and around. The right heel moves further up as the body keeps turning.

**The finish** The body completes its forward turn in response to the club's momentum. Ossie's arms have swung up and around. The hips are facing the target. He is in total balance.

| THE SIT POSITION | APPROACHING LATE RELEASE | FOLLOW THROUGH | THE CROSSOVER | THE FINISH |

# OSSIE MOORE

**Address** Front on you see Ossie's ball position is close to centre — *not the front heel*. I recommend this ball placement to most golfers. Ossie has a somewhat narrow stance. This, combined with excess knee bend, means he has to rely on a smooth tempo to stay in dynamic balance. Note the higher left shoulder, extended left arm and relaxed bent right arm.

**Takeaway** This photo was taken slightly after the one above and here we see the wrists starting to hinge in response to the swinging club. Note how the arms hang low and there is no picking up of the club.

**Waist high** Front on you can see the swinging club has stretched the left arm straight and the left shoulder is being pulled back and around. One of the strengths in Ossie's swing is his ability to load his wrists to help wind up his backswing. Ossie is turning around his right foot as axis. The left heel is being dragged off the ground. The head is steady.

**At the top** Note how the hips have turned left, moving the left knee and left foot. Both feet are solidly planted in the ground. The shoulders, arms, wrists and club have been dragged around and down. There is still great coil of the shoulders against the hips and the arms against the shoulders. The wrists are fully loaded.

**Impact** Head steady, hands ahead of ball, wrists uncocked, right elbow still slightly bent. Weight solidly planted on left foot. Left shoulder high. Right shoulder low.

ADDRESS    TAKEAWAY    WAIST HIGH    AT THE TOP    START DOWN

**Releasing** Here the wrists are beginning to uncock as the hands reach the bottom of their downward motion. The head is steady and left side relatively firm.

**Follow through** Both arms are straight. The right shoulder is down, the left shoulder high, the head steady. The hips have dragged the right foot off the ground. The right knee is being dragged in and forward.

**The crossover** Into the finish the momentum of the swinging club is dragging Ossie's arms, shoulders, hips, legs and right foot up and around. The head is gradually moving up and around to follow the flight of the ball.

**The finish** Note the full turn, the weight on the left side, the firm left side and the balance. Ossie's grip has remained unaltered.

THE SIT POSITION    APPROACHING LATE RELEASE    FOLLOW THROUGH    THE CROSSOVER    THE FINISH

# DAVID GRAHAM

David Graham is a true professional all the way. He developed his swing through learning the fundamentals with persistent hard work over many years. His two major championships, the U.S. Open and USPGA titles are part of the reward for his efforts.

In his early days as a professional in Melbourne he played left handed. He changed over and I believe his early experiences left handed have not hurt his overall feel for the swing.

David has helped many others to greater achievement, including Greg Norman.

**Address** David has a solid, shoulder width stance, feet flat on the ground. Ball position centre. Left arm straight. Solid two knuckle grip.

**The takeaway** A one piece takeaway — the hip turn has moved the shoulders, arms, hands and club away in a wide arc. The weight is moving to the right side.

**Around waist high** The weight has shifted to the right side by now. The wrists have cocked, stretching the left arm and beginning to fold the right. Note the coiling of the hips has dragged the left knee back.

**Top of backswing** Full body coil, straight left arm and flat shoulder turn. Weight on right side.

**Approaching late release** Weight has been transferred dynamically to the left side. The left hip is turning left into the left heel. The left arm is extended. The head has moved slightly down and forward.

ADDRESS　　　　THE TAKEAWAY　　　　AROUND WAIST HIGH　　　　TOP OF BACKSWING

**Impact** Here David's weight is 99% on the left side. He has released his hands and his body against the ball.

**The crossover** Here the swinging club has crossed over the forearms. The right foot has moved up as the hip turns fully left.

**The finish** Here the body has moved up to a balanced finish. The weight is totally over to the left side.

APPROACHING LATE
RELEASE

IMPACT

CROSSOVER

FINISH

# DAVID GRAHAM

**Address** Feet parallel to target line. Good posture with knees slightly flexed. The lower body is in solid balance.

**The takeaway** Note the left knee has moved in response to the hip turn. The club shaft is an extension of the left arm. The left hand has turned under slightly to flatten the left wrist. The hands are passive at this stage. The right knee is flexed.

**Around waist high** The club shaft is on the swing plane and note how David's left knee has been dragged in and back. The left arm is fully extended and David's head remains at a constant height.

**Top of backswing** The club shaft is on the swing plane. The right elbow points down, the back of the left wrist is flat. The weight is shown to be in balance on the right foot. Head is kept at constant height.

**Approaching late release** The left hip has cleared sharply left. The hands have moved positively down, towards late release. The right elbow has moved close into the side. David is in dynamic balance.

**Impact** The hips have cleared to the left. The shoulders are near square to the target line.

ADDRESS      THE TAKEAWAY      AROUND WAIST HIGH      TOP OF BACKSWING

**The crossover** The shoulders are beginning to turn left and the hand is moving up and forward.

**The finish** The left side has totally cleared and the body faces left of target. Note the club, hands and arms have swung to the left with the turn.

APPROACHING LATE
RELEASE

IMPACT

CROSSOVER

FINISH

THE TAKEAWAY      ABOVE WAIST HIGH      TOP OF BACKSWING      START DOWN      APPROACHING LATE RELEASE

# GREG NORMAN

Greg Norman has developed into one of the world's super stars and his dynamic power game, plus a healthy self confidence, are contributing factors to his great success. I have known him since school days in Townsville, North Queensland.

There is no doubt that he modelled himself on Jack Nicklaus at an early age. He, as Nicklaus has done, has refined his swing to bring his arm action into closer co-ordination with his body coil, thus flattening his swing plane considerably since his early days on the professional circuit. His unusual foot action of a few years back has been contained by a better address set up and a more down the line swing path.

In summary, Greg has a great swing but one which demands a strong and supple body. I think Greg will find ways of minimising the strains in critical areas over the coming years, just as Nicklaus has done.

**The takeaway** Here Greg is well into the start-up. His body turn has allowed his arms, hands and club to swing back in a one piece movement. Greg's key to his backswing is R.P.B. (right pocket back). His last three fingers of his left hand have turned under slightly to give him a slightly closed club face and a flat left wrist. Note the left knee has been dragged out and back. The right knee is still flexed. The feet are both flat and heavy in the ground. The head is steady and the eyes are on the ball.

**Above wrist high** Here the wrists have cocked and the right elbow is folding. The left wrist is flat. The left arm is extended. The hip turn is greater and Greg has the feeling of sitting on his right side. The right knee has remained flexed. The left knee has been dragged further out and around. The head is steady and the eyes are on the ball. Note the left shoulder is moving more *around* than *under*. Greg is solid in his feet and in perfect dynamic balance.

**Top of backswing** Greg has full coil, a powerful position. The hips are fully wound against the feet, the wrists are fully cocked, the arms are wound against the shoulders and the shoulders are wound against the hips. Note the right elbow, although away from his side, is pointing downward. The left arm is fully

IMPACT       FOLLOW THROUGH       INTO FOLLOW THROUGH       THE FINISH

extended. The arm swing is more upright than the shoulder turn, thus the upper arm covers the chin. The head is steady and the eyes are still over the ball. This backswing position is much lower than when Greg first started on the tour. Now his arm swing is in much closer harmony with his body.

**Start down** The downswing has been started by Greg's left hip turning back into his left heel. Note the left knee has responded by moving forward and left. Both feet are planted solidly in the ground. Both knees are still flexed. The hands have been pulled down towards the ball. The right elbow has compressed down and in toward the right hip. The left wrist is still flat. Head steady and eyes on the ball. Left arm fully extended. The right shoulder is moving downward.

**Approaching late release** Here the left hip moves further left. The left shoulder has resisted slightly and the right shoulder and elbow have moved down and under, bringing the hands down low toward the ball. This has created maximum wrist cock and an extremely late release. Both feet are solidly in the ground and Greg's head has remained steady and his eyes are on the ball.

**Impact** Here Greg is unloading all his power on the ball. Both feet are solidly in the ground and the further hip turn has moved the weight to the inside of the right foot, rolling it over. The head is steady and eyes are on the ball. Shoulders are nearly square to the line of flight. Left arm is straight. Right arm is still bent and note the shaft and right forearm are in the same plane of action. The right shoulder is moving under his chin. Note the upright shoulder action in the downswing.

**Follow through** Greg's right arm has fully extended. The right shoulder has moved under the chin. The head is beginning to move up and around to follow the flight of the ball. The right foot is being dragged out of the ground and the right knee is moving in response to the hip turn.

**Into the follow through** Here the momentum of the swinging club has pulled Greg's arms, shoulders, hips, right knee and foot, up and around. His head is moving up towards the finish position. Note the roll into the left heel.

**The finish** A totally released position. Greg has held nothing back. The body has fully unwound. He still has a firm grip of the club and has finished in balance.